C U T A W A Y
TRUCKS

JON KIRKWOOD

COPPER BEECH BOOKS

BROOKFIELD, CONNECTICUT

*Designed and
produced by*
Aladdin Books Ltd
28 Percy Street
London W1P 0LD

*First published in the
United States in 1997 by*
Copper Beech Books,
an imprint of
The Millbrook Press
2 Old New Milford Road
Brookfield, Connecticut
06804

Editor
Jon Richards
Consultant
Steve Allman
Design
David West Children's
Book Design
Designer
Robert Perry
Illustrators
Simon Tegg & Graham White
Picture Research
Brooks Krikler Research

Printed in Belgium

**Library of Congress
Cataloging-in-Publication Data**

Kirkwood, Jon.
Trucks / Jon Kirkwood ; illustrated
by Simon Tegg and Graham White
p. cm. — (Cutaway)
Includes index.
Summary: Examines different types
of trucks, how they work, how
they are used, and the people
who drive them.
ISBN 0-7613-0641-2 (pb).
— ISBN 0-7613-0710-9 (lib.bdg.)
1. Trucks—Juvenile literature.
[1.Trucks.] I. Tegg, Simon, ill.
II. Title III. Series
TL230.15K57 1997   97-24337
629.224—dc21   CIP AC

CONTENTS

INTRODUCTION

Trucks are vital for our way of life. They carry large loads from place to place. Trucks with cranes also let us lift objects high into the air with the greatest of ease.

There are trucks for other important jobs. They can mix concrete,

carry logs, dig holes, race each other at high speeds, do stunts, and even swim rivers.

TRACTOR UNIT

The front parts of trucks that bend in the middle are called tractor units. Drivers sit inside the cabs at the front of the tractor units. From here, they can steer the trucks along the road. Some cabs may even have beds in the back (*see* pages 16-17)!

Beneath the cab is the engine. This needs to be very powerful to drive the tractor unit and pull its load. This engine is as strong as the engines from ten small cars!

Trailer link
Behind the cab is a device that links the tractor unit to a trailer. This special link lets the articulated truck bend in the middle. The truck can then turn very tight corners.

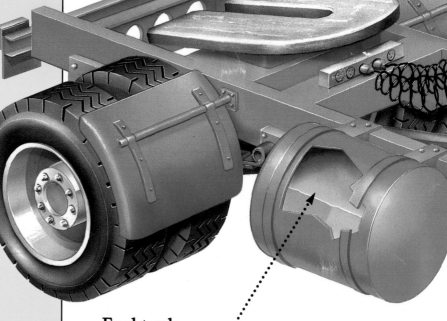

Fuel tank
The fuel tank contains the fuel for the tractor unit's engine.

Wheels
A tractor unit has two or more sets of wheels. The front set steers the tractor unit. The rear sets push the tractor unit along and carry the weight of the trailer.

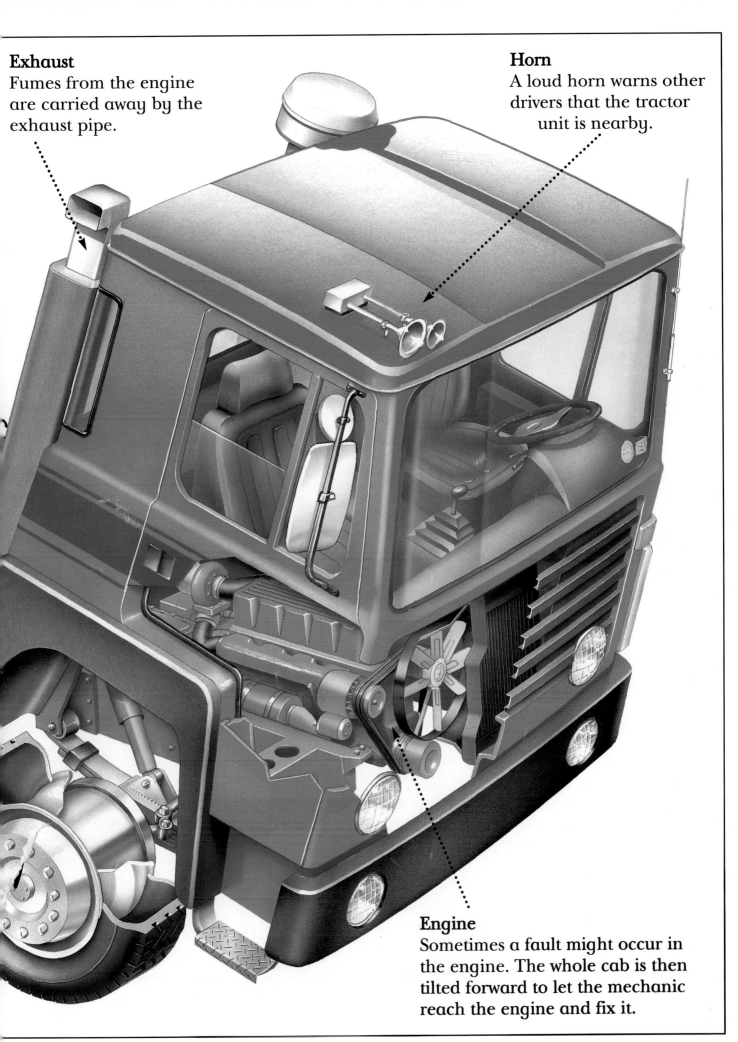

Exhaust
Fumes from the engine are carried away by the exhaust pipe.

Horn
A loud horn warns other drivers that the tractor unit is nearby.

Engine
Sometimes a fault might occur in the engine. The whole cab is then tilted forward to let the mechanic reach the engine and fix it.

Trucks come in all

Funnel

Boiler

Wheel

Steering wheel

Steam-powered truck

Early trucks (*above*) used steam engines instead of diesel engines. Water was heated in a boiler to make steam that gave the power to drive the truck.

Pick up

One of the most popular types of truck has been the pick up truck (*right*). Behind the cab is a flat bed where the load is carried.

shapes and sizes.

One-piece trucks

Some trucks come in one piece (*below*). At the front of the truck is the cab where the drivers sit. Behind this, the truck is fitted with one type of body unit. This could be a rubbish compactor, a crane, or a container.

Container

Articulated trucks

Some trucks have trailers that are pulled by a tractor unit. Between the tractor unit and the trailer is a special device that allows the truck to bend. These trucks are called articulated trucks. Sometimes, a tractor unit may pull more than one trailer (*right*).

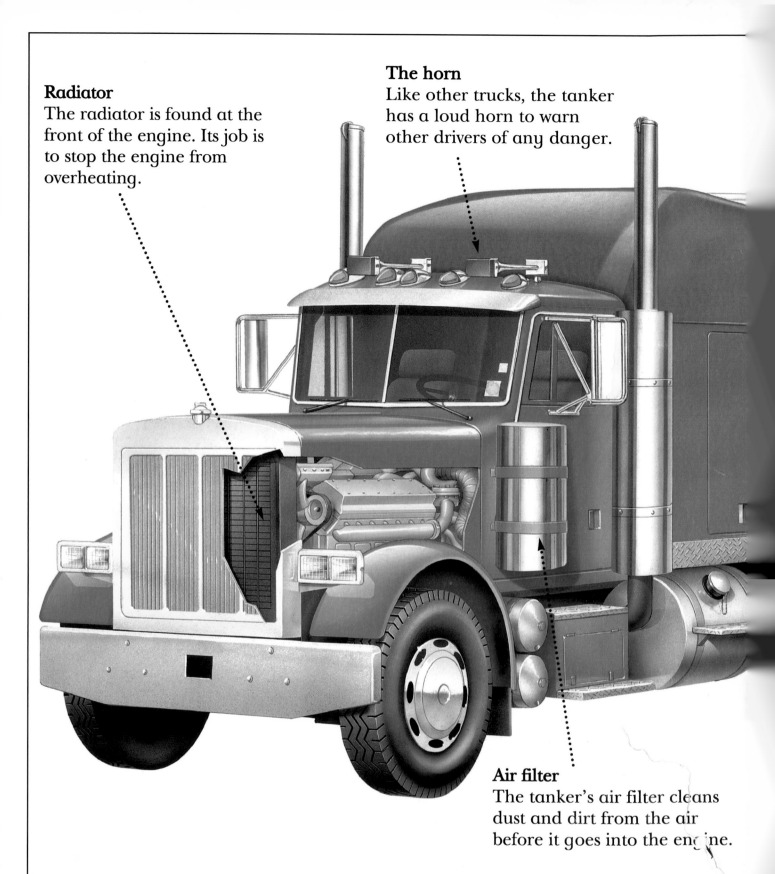

Radiator
The radiator is found at the front of the engine. Its job is to stop the engine from overheating.

The horn
Like other trucks, the tanker has a loud horn to warn other drivers of any danger.

Air filter
The tanker's air filter cleans dust and dirt from the air before it goes into the engine.

TANKER

Tankers pull special types of trailers. These trailers are designed to carry liquids, such as gasoline and milk.

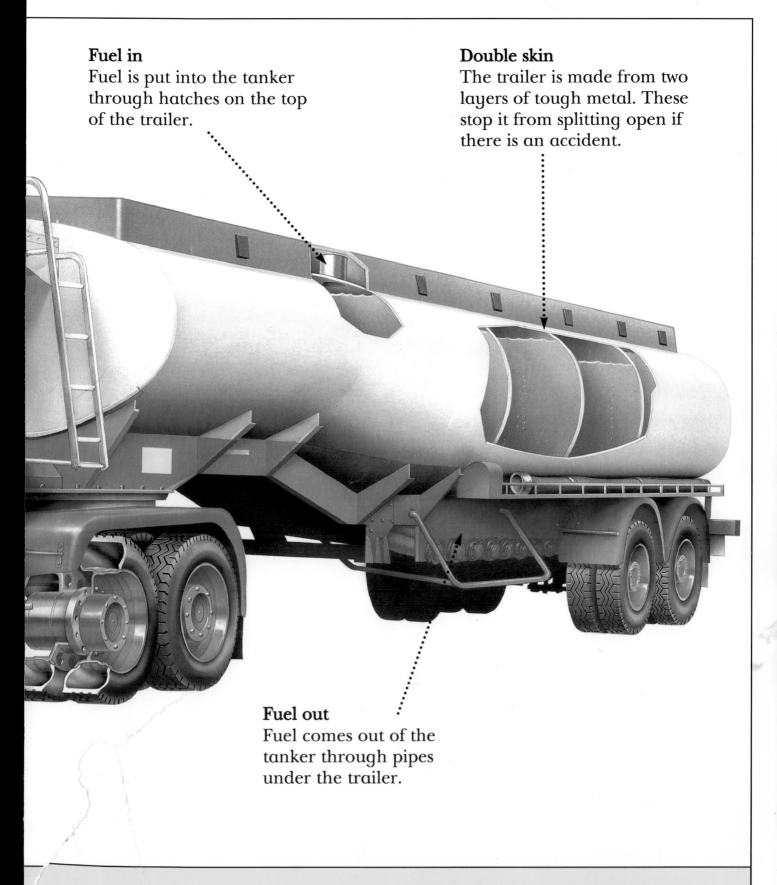

Fuel in
Fuel is put into the tanker through hatches on the top of the trailer.

Double skin
The trailer is made from two layers of tough metal. These stop it from splitting open if there is an accident.

Fuel out
Fuel comes out of the tanker through pipes under the trailer.

A fuel tanker is filled with either gasoline or diesel at the storage depot. The tanker then carries its load to gas stations.

Here the fuel is pumped out of the tanker and into storage tanks. These storage tanks are usually kept underground.

Trailers are used to

Low-loader

A truck that can bend between the trailer and the tractor unit is called an articulated truck. Sometimes, they may be fitted with a very low trailer, called a low-loader. These are designed to carry very heavy or very large loads (*above* and *right*).

Heavy load

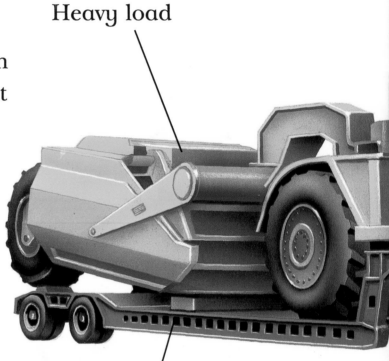

Low trailer

Logging truck

Some articulated trucks carry logs (*left*). Here, sets of wheels are fixed to either end of the logs. The logs and wheels together act as a trailer.

carry heavy loads.

More than one

To carry a lot of cargo, more than one trailer may be used, as with a road-train. These make the truck very long (*right*).

Cab

Car transporter

Some trailers are made to carry cars. These trailers have two or even three decks. This means that one articulated truck can carry eleven cars at one time (*below*).

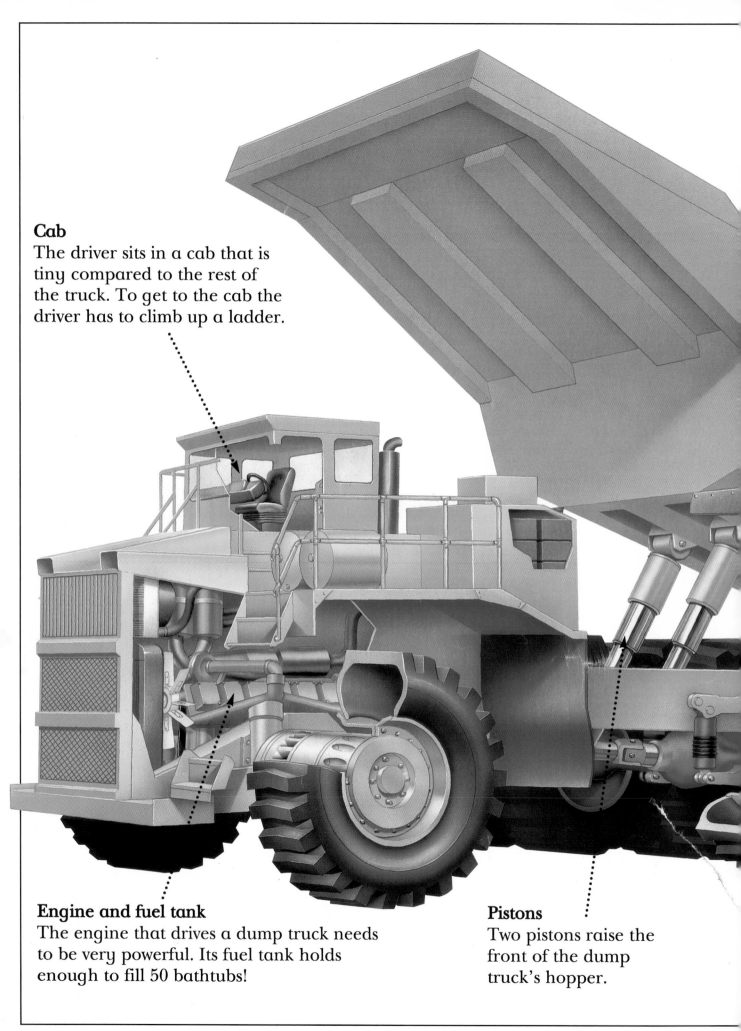

Cab
The driver sits in a cab that is tiny compared to the rest of the truck. To get to the cab the driver has to climb up a ladder.

Engine and fuel tank
The engine that drives a dump truck needs to be very powerful. Its fuel tank holds enough to fill 50 bathtubs!

Pistons
Two pistons raise the front of the dump truck's hopper.

Hopper
Some dump trucks can carry loads that weigh as much as 70 elephants. When it is tipping out its load, the top of the hopper can reach as high as a five-story building!

DUMP TRUCK

Quarries and mines are places where massive amounts of rock are dug from the ground by enormous digging machines called excavators. Huge dump trucks are needed to carry the rocks away. The excavators empty the rocks into a container at the back of the dump truck. This container is called the hopper. The truck then drives to where the load is to be dumped. When it reaches the site, two pistons push the front of the hopper up. The rocks then simply slide out of the back of the hopper.

Wheels
This dump truck has huge wheels. Each one is more than the height of two adults!

Trucks do a lot of

Concrete mixer

Concrete is carried to a building site in a concrete mixer (*below*). This has a mixing drum on the back that turns slowly to mix the concrete. When it reaches the site, concrete is poured out through the delivery chute.

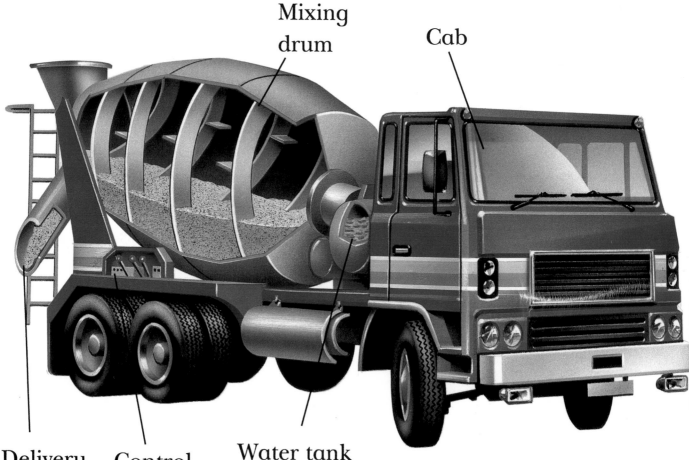

Mixing drum

Cab

Delivery chute

Control panel

Water tank

Pumper truck

Sometimes, concrete has to be pumped up to high places from a concrete mixer. When this happens a special pumper truck (*left*) is used.

jobs on building sites.

Tipper truck

A tipper truck (*left*) carries loads or containers. When the truck reaches the site where the cargo is needed, the rear tilts up and the cargo slides off.

Loader

Loaders (*right*) are fitted with huge shovels on the front. They are used to scoop up piles of rocks and earth and dump them in the back of other trucks.

Scraper

These large trucks (*left*) are used to move large amounts of earth. Underneath the truck is a large blade that skims along the ground, digging up the top layer of the soil.

What it takes to

Inside the cab

Driving a truck is a tough job to do. Truck drivers may spend many hours on the road. To make their lives as easy as possible, trucks are built with many of the comforts of home (*right*).

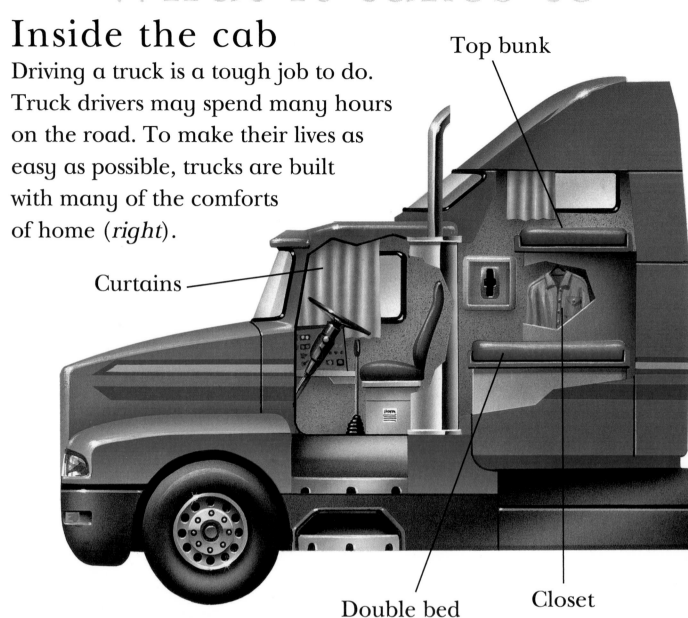

Top bunk

Curtains

Double bed

Closet

Instrument panel

The instrument panels on the dashboard (*left*) give the driver information about the truck. The panel includes dials showing speed, the distance traveled, engine temperature, and fuel level.

be a truck driver.

Living area

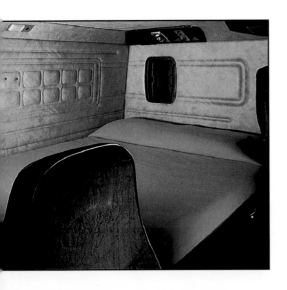

In some cabs there are living quarters for the driver to use. There may be a bed (*left*) and washing facilities including a shower. Some trucks have a small kitchen with a refrigerator, and a relaxation area, perhaps with a desk for doing paperwork.

Suspension

A truck's wheels are fitted with springs and pistons (*right*). These make the ride very smooth for the driver.

Smooth body

The shape of a tractor unit is built to be smooth (*left*). This helps it slip through the air as easily as possible. As a result, the truck uses less fuel, and can carry loads farther.

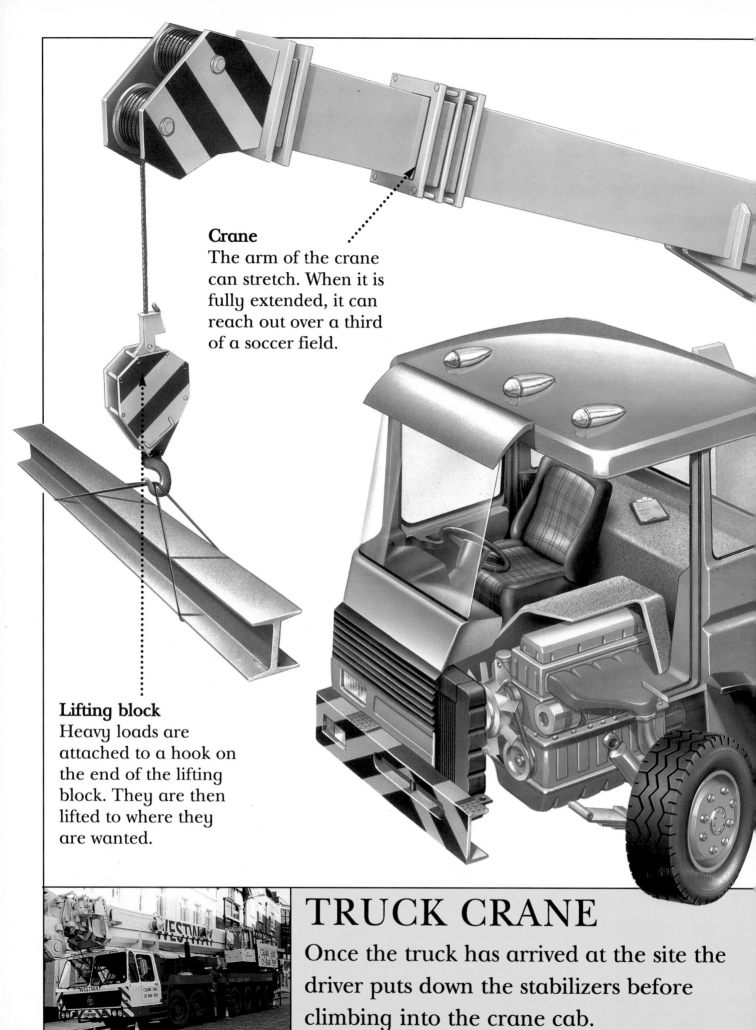

Crane
The arm of the crane can stretch. When it is fully extended, it can reach out over a third of a soccer field.

Lifting block
Heavy loads are attached to a hook on the end of the lifting block. They are then lifted to where they are wanted.

TRUCK CRANE

Once the truck has arrived at the site the driver puts down the stabilizers before climbing into the crane cab.

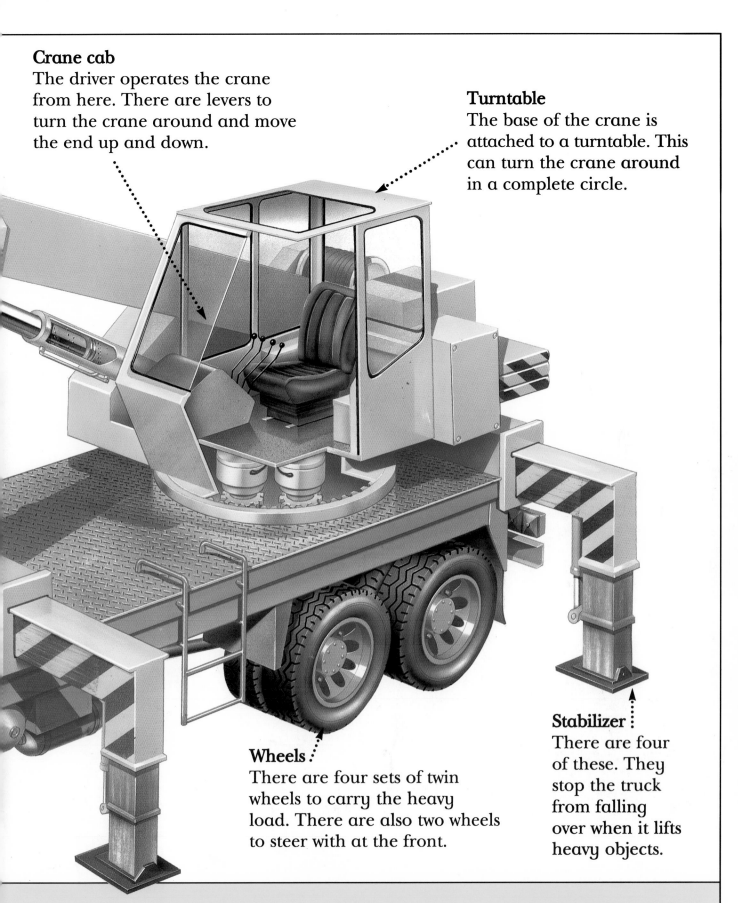

Crane cab
The driver operates the crane from here. There are levers to turn the crane around and move the end up and down.

Turntable
The base of the crane is attached to a turntable. This can turn the crane around in a complete circle.

Stabilizer
There are four of these. They stop the truck from falling over when it lifts heavy objects.

Wheels
There are four sets of twin wheels to carry the heavy load. There are also two wheels to steer with at the front.

Once in the cab the driver can operate the crane. A telescopic arm moves the crane in and out. A piston moves the arm up and down. The truck crane has two diesel engines. One is used to power the truck while the other powers the crane.

Trucks can pick up

Fork lift truck

A fork lift truck has two forks at the front. These forks are placed under a load to lift it. The strongest fork lift trucks can lift a load that weighs as much as 15 elephants.

Lifting forks

Engine

Cherry picker

A cherry-picker truck (*left*) has a platform at the end of an arm. This arm stretches up to reach high above the ground. The whole truck is kept steady by four stabilizers (*see* page 19).

big and small loads.

Heavy-lift crane

When very large loads need lifting, a heavy-lift crane (*right*) is used. These huge trucks can have ten sets of wheels. The huge arm of the crane can stretch almost the length of a soccer field. As with a smaller truck crane (*see* pages 18-19), this crane uses stabilizers to keep it steady.

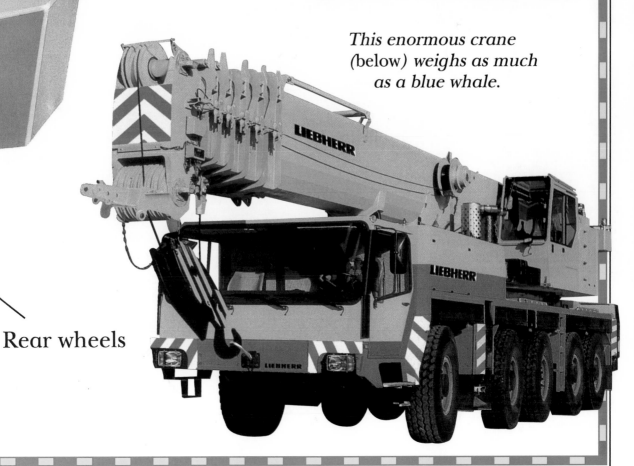

This enormous crane (below) weighs as much as a blue whale.

Rear wheels

SWIMMING TRUCK

Some special trucks are able to swim across lakes and rivers. They are call amphibious trucks. When they travel over the ground, they are driven by their wheels, just like normal trucks. However, when they enter the water, propellers spin to push the amphibious truck along.

This amphibious truck (*right*) is used by the army to carry other vehicles, such as tanks, across a river. It can also be used to build bridges across rivers. Several of these trucks swim alongside each other to form the bridge. They can build a bridge as long as a soccer field in only 20 minutes.

Engine
The engine is at the rear of the vehicle. It drives the vehicle over land and turns the propeller when it is "swimming."

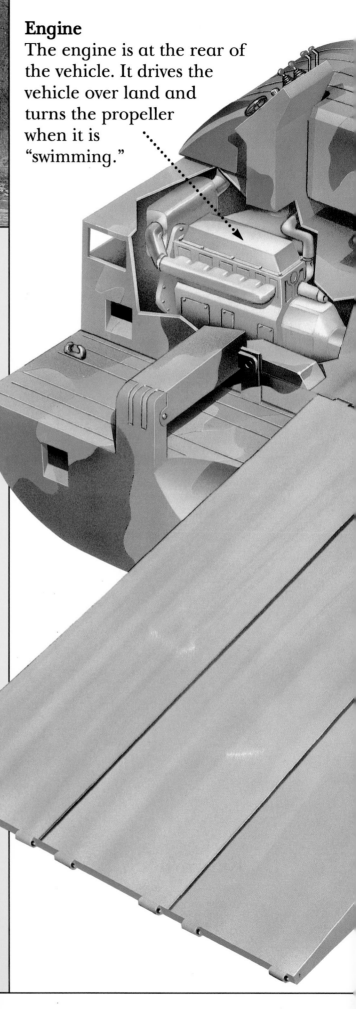

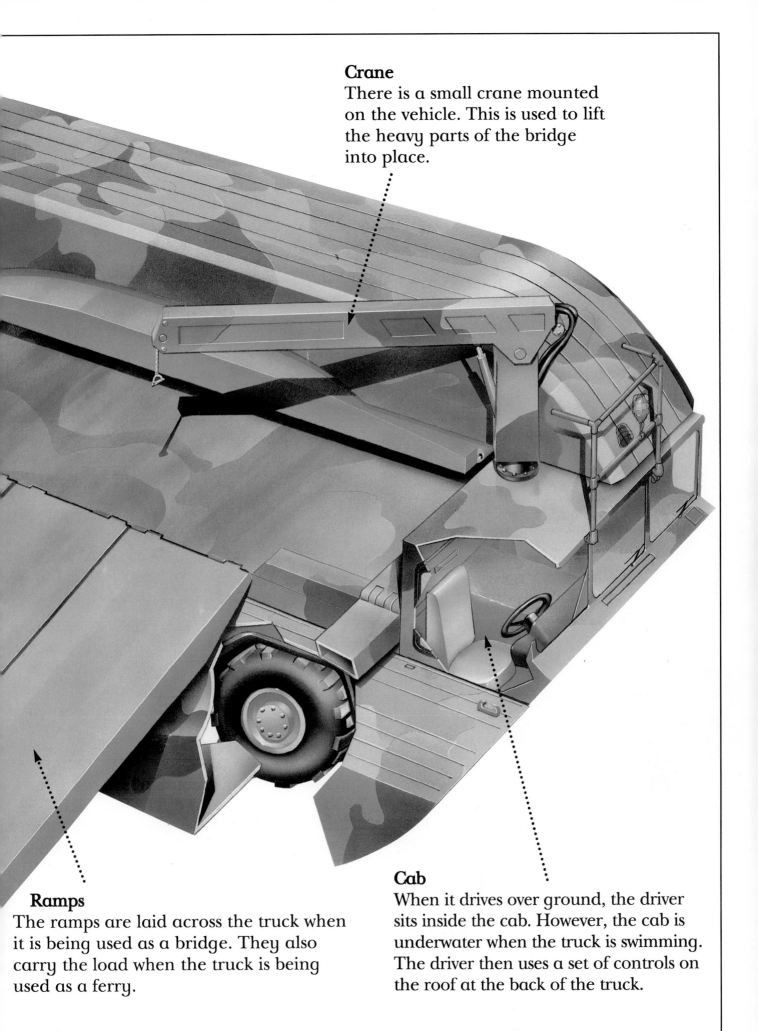

Crane
There is a small crane mounted on the vehicle. This is used to lift the heavy parts of the bridge into place.

Ramps
The ramps are laid across the truck when it is being used as a bridge. They also carry the load when the truck is being used as a ferry.

Cab
When it drives over ground, the driver sits inside the cab. However, the cab is underwater when the truck is swimming. The driver then uses a set of controls on the roof at the back of the truck.

Some trucks don't

Armored vehicles

This armored car (*right*) weighed as much as five elephants! It was equipped with a gun and had armor to protect the soldiers inside. Armored trucks are used to carry equipment and soldiers around a battlefield.

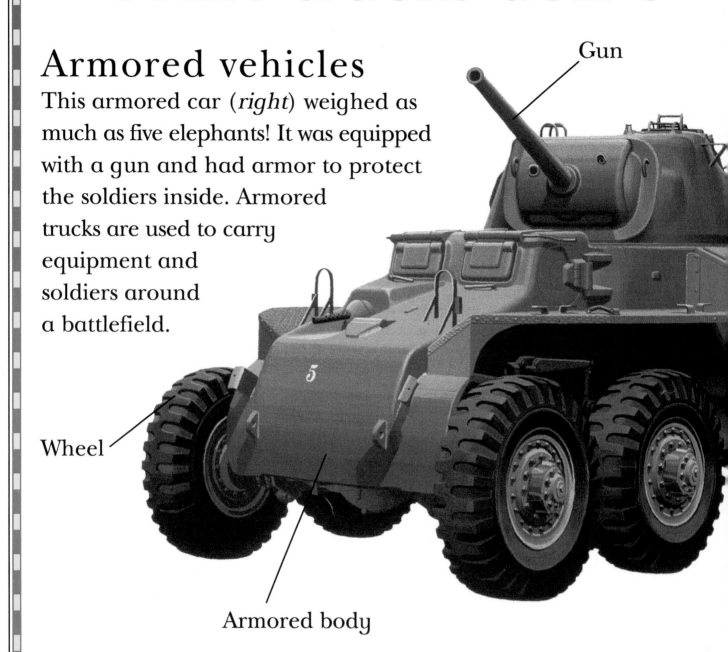

Gun

Wheel

Armored body

Trucks on tracks

This truck (*left*) is used to carry out repairs on railroads. It is fitted with special wheels, called bogies, that allow the truck to drive along the rail tracks.

always drive on roads.

Desert trucks

Some trucks have to drive through the desert (*right*). To cope with the rough ground they need tough suspension (*see* page 17) and large tires.

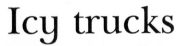

Icy trucks

Trucks that drive over ice and snow use extra-wide wheels that are fitted with special snow tires (*below*). These tires give the truck extra grip and stop it from sliding about. They also stop the truck from sinking into the snow.

Cab

Cabs are equipped with special safety cages
to protect the drivers. They also have
safety harnesses to stop the drivers
from being thrown
around.

Engine

Racing trucks are equipped with
very powerful engines. These can
be twice as powerful as a normal
tractor-unit engine!

Body work
Some racing trucks are fitted with extra body parts. These help the trucks drive faster by letting them move through the air as easily as possible.

RACING TRUCK

Racing trucks are tractor units that are altered to make them go faster. These trucks race each other around race tracks. They are equipped with more powerful engines, allowing them to go much faster than normal trucks. Lightweight materials are used throughout the truck to make it as light as possible. Even the glass of the windows and windshield is replaced. These new materials also have to be strong to protect the driver if there is a crash.

Brakes
Racing trucks have brakes that get very hot during racing. They are cooled with water to stop them from getting too hot.

Some other jobs

Tow truck

Sometimes a car or a truck breaks down and cannot drive any farther. When this happens a tow truck (*below*) will attach a hook to the vehicle and lift one end. The tow truck then pulls the broken vehicle to a garage where it can be fixed.

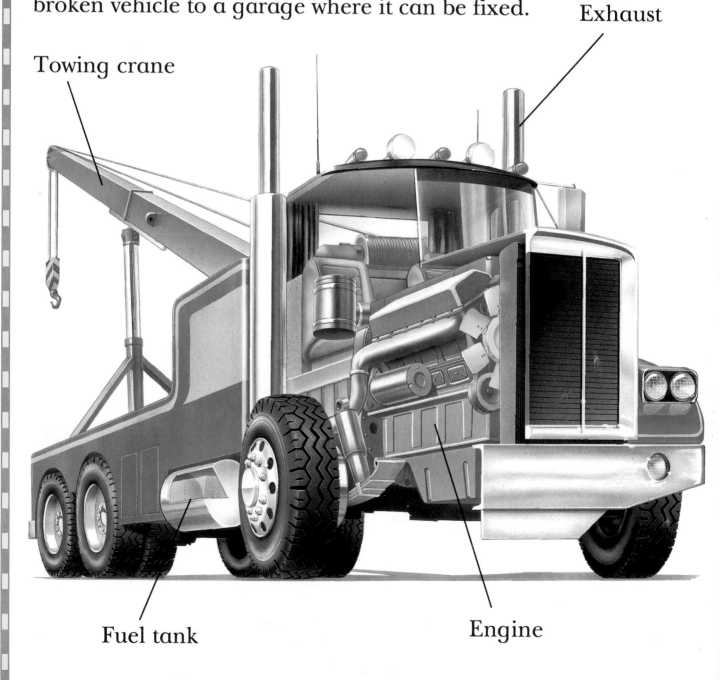

Towing crane

Exhaust

Fuel tank

Engine

that trucks do.

Racing team

These trucks (*right*) carry the cars and equipment for a motor racing team. At the end of the race, the trucks are loaded up and then driven off to the next event.

Fun trucks

Many trucks are altered to do special stunts. Some of them can do wheelies (*left*). Other trucks, called monster trucks, have huge wheels and crush other cars when they drive over them (*below*).

Fantastic Facts

• The first truck was built in 1769 by the Frenchman Nicolas-Joseph Cugnot. It was powered by steam and was built to pull cannons into battle. However, it lost control during testing and was never used again.

• The longest truck in the world was an Australian road-train. Pulling five trailers, this truck was as long as 15 cars, weighed as much as 150 cars, and had 110 wheels!

• The most powerful tow truck in the world is called the "Hulk." It can pull the weight of two blue whales!

• The fastest truck in the world is powered by three jet-fighter engines and can drive at 256 mph (412 km/h)!

Glossary

Amphibious truck
A road truck that can also swim. Its engine drives both the wheels and a propeller.

Articulated truck
A truck that comes in two or more parts. At the front is the tractor unit that pulls one or more trailers.

Bogies
These are special wheels that are built to run on rail tracks.

Cherry picker
A truck that has a platform on the end of an arm. This arm can extend, lifting the platform to high places.

Diesel
A type of fuel that is used in truck and car engines.

Suspension
A system of springs and other devices that smooth the ride of a truck.

Tractor unit
The front part of an articulated truck. The driver sits in the tractor unit to drive the truck. It also contains the engine.

Trailer
Towed behind a truck or tractor unit, the trailer is the part that carries the load or cargo.

Index

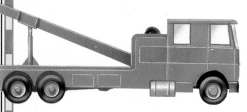

PHOTO CREDITS
Abbreviations: t-top, m-middle, b-bottom, r-right, l-left, c-center.
Pages 4, 13, 15m – Roger Vlitos. 6 – Zefa. 7t – Foden/Paccar.
7b, 10b, 11t, 14, 15t, 16, 17t & m – Peterbilt/Paccar. 8, 15b, 18 –
Spectrum Colour Library. 10t – Caterpillar. 11b, 25t, 27,
29m – Eye Ubiquitous. 17b – Kenworth Truck
Company. 20, 21 both, 24 – Liebherr. 22 – EWK.
25b – James Davis Travel Photography.
29t – Renault. 29b – Frank Spooner Pictures.